EASY RENAISSANCE MUS[...]

LEICHTE RENAISSANCEMU[...]

MUSIQUE RENAISSANCE LÉGÈRE

KÖNNYŰ RENESZÁNSZ MUZSIKA

for Guitar – für Gitarre – pour guitare – gitárra

Transcribed and edited by – Bearbeitet und herausgegeben von
Arrangé et édité par – Átírta és közreadja

MOSÓCZI Miklós

EDITIO MUSICA BUDAPEST

Universal Music Publishing Editio Musica Budapest Ltd
H-1370 Budapest, P.O.B. 322 • Tel.: (361) 236-1100 • Telefax: (361) 236-1101
E-mail: emb@emb.hu • Internet: http://www.emb.hu
© Copyright 2011 by Editio Musica Budapest
Printed in Hungary

CONTENTS – INHALT – TABLE – TARTALOM

Corranto

Anon.

Corranto

Anon.

Z. 14 733

Watkins Ale

Anon.

Pavane et Galliarde Ferrarese

Galliarde

Balletto „Spagnoletto"

Anon.

Balletto „La Fedeltà d'Amore"

Anon.

Ein ungerischer Tantz

Wolff HECKEL
(ca 1515–1562)

Ungaresca

Anon.

Saltarello

Allemande

Anon.

Kemp's Jig

Anon.

Danza

Anon.

Wir lieben sehr im Herzen

Daniel FRIDERICI
(1584–1638)

Can Shee

Anon.

A Gigge, Doctor Bulls My selfe

John BULL
(1562/3–1628)

Playfellow Jig

Antony HOLBORNE
(ca 1545–1602)

Muscadin

Anon.

The Fall of the Leafe

Martin PEERSON
(1571/73–1651)

Tanz und Nachtanz

Valentin HAUSSMANN
(ca 1560 – ca 1611/13)

All Lust und Freud

Hans Leo HASSLER
(1564–1612)

Tourdion

Anon.

Fine

Da Capo al Fine

Ronde et Saltarelle

Tylman SUSATO
(1510/15–1570)

Allemande

Anon.

Balletto „Alba Novella"

Fabritio CAROSO
(1527/35 – after/nach/après 1605 után)

Balletto „Pavaniglia"

Fabritio CAROSO

Balletto „Il Conto dell'Orco"

Fabritio CAROSO

Balletto „Alta Mendozza"

Anon.

Der Fuggerin Dantz

Melchior NEUSIDLER
(1531–1590)

Greensleeves

Anon.

Ein niderlendisch Tentzlein

Hans NEUSIDLER
(ca 1508/9–1563)

Ein Welscher Tanz „Wascha mesa"

Hans NEUSIDLER

Der Hupff auff

Felelős kiadó a Universal Music Publishing
Editio Musica Budapest Zeneműkiadó Kft. igazgatója
Z. 14 733 (4,2 A5 ív) 2011/77065, AduPrint Nyomda Kft., Budapest
Felelős vezető: Tóth Béláné ügyvezető igazgató
Felelős szerkesztő: Soós András – Műszaki szerkesztő: Metzker Sándor
A kottagrafikát Dénesné Lukács Marian készítette
Printed in Hungary

WORKS FOR GUITAR / GITÁRMŰVEK
Collections / Gyűjtemények

Git/6

ISMN 979 0 080 14733 7

DISTRIBUTED BY
HAL LEONARD
CORPORATION

50490594